THE
21 SUCCESS
SECRETS OF
$ELF-MADE
MILLIONAIRE$

THE
21 SUCCESS SECRETS OF
$ELF-MADE MILLIONAIRE$

HOW TO ACHIEVE FINANCIAL INDEPENDENCE FASTER AND EASIER THAN YOU EVER THOUGHT POSSIBLE

BRIAN TRACY

BERRETT–KOEHLER PUBLISHERS, INC.
San Francisco

Executive Books
205 West Allen Street
Mechanicsburg, PA 17055

Tel: (800) 233-2565
Fax: (717) 766-6565
www.executivebooks.com

Printed in the United States of America

 Printed on acid-free and recycled paper that is composed
of 50% recovered fiber, including 10% postconsumer waste.

Library of Congress Cataloging-in-Publication Data
Tracy, Brian.
21 success secrets of self-made millionaires / by Brian Tracy.
    p. cm.
ISBN 1-57675-158-9 (pbk.)
    1. Success in business.   2. Millionaires.   I. Title: Twenty-one
success secrets of self-made millionaires.   II. Title.
    HF5386.T8137   2000
    332.024'01—dc21   00-011248

Copyediting and proofreading by Peoplespeak.
Book design and composition by Beverly Butterfield, Girl of the West Productions.
This edition published by arrangement with Berrett-Koehler Publishers, Inc.

FIRST EDITION

05 04   03   02   01   10   9   8   7   6   5   4   3   2

Contents

Preface

This book is the culmination of 15 years of research, teaching, and personal experience on the subject of self-made millionaires. These pages contain the key ideas and strategies I have discovered in reading hundreds of books and thousands of articles on the subject of wealth accumulation. The ideas and strategies are presented in a simple, tested, proven, easy-to-use format so that you can learn and apply them immediately.

When I was a teenager growing up in Pomona, California, in a home where we never had very much money, my dream, my fantasy, was to be a millionaire by the time I was 30. Lots of people have the same dream, I'm sure.

However, when I reached the age of 30, I was still just as broke as when I was 20. Then I did something that changed my life. I began asking, Why are some people more successful than others? I especially wanted to know, How is it that some people start off with nothing and eventually become millionaires?

This question set me off on a search for the answers, which has led to this book.

I chose self-made millionaires as my focal point because these people had demonstrated special qualities and behaviors that were both observable and measurable. They had started with nothing and passed the magic million-dollar mark as the result of doing certain things in a certain way, over and over.

What I learned was that in order to achieve great success in life, you must become a special kind of person. To rise above the majority, you must develop qualities and disciplines that the average person lacks.

The most important factor in achieving great financial success is not the money. It is the kind of person you have to become to earn that money and then hold on to it.

These 21 "success secrets" are the keys to great success in every area of life, whether or not you make a lot of money. The good news is that these principles are so powerful that you can apply them to accomplish almost anything you really want. Many of these methods and techniques will seem familiar to you. This is because they have been discovered and rediscovered for hundreds of years. I see myself more as a student of success—a reader, a researcher, a synthesizer, and a teacher of great ideas—than as an originator or creator of brand new concepts. I believe, as it says in Ecclesiastes, "There is nothing new under the sun."

Since you are reading this book, I know that one of your great goals in life is to become an extraordinary person, to realize more and more of your true potential. Each of these success secrets will help you to move ahead more rapidly toward the wonderful life that is possible for you. Enjoy the journey!

BRIAN TRACY
August 2000

To my wonderful son, David,
a fine student, a great entrepreneur,
and a self-made millionaire of the future

Introduction:
The Law of Cause
and Effect

What you are about to learn can change your life. These ideas, insights, and strategies have been the springboards to financial success for millions of men and women, young and old, rich and poor. These principles are simple, effective, and fairly easy to apply. They have been tested and proven over and over again, and they will work for you if you will take them and apply them in your own life.

We are living at the greatest time in all of human history. More people are becoming wealthy today, starting from nothing, than ever before imagined. There are more than seven million millionaires in America, most of them self-made, and the number is growing by 15 to 20 percent each year. We even have self-made ten millionaires, hundred millionaires, and more than two hundred billionaires. We have never seen this type of rapid wealth creation in all of human history.

Here's the best news of all. Virtually everyone starts with nothing. More than 90 percent of all financially successful people today started off broke or nearly broke. The average self-made millionaire has been bankrupt or nearly bankrupt 3.2 times. Most wealthy people failed many times before they finally found the right opportunity that they were able to leverage into financial success. And what hundreds of thousands and millions of other people have done, you can do as well.

The iron law of human destiny is the Law of Cause and Effect. This law is simple yet very powerful. It says that there is a specific effect for every cause. For every action, there is a reaction. This law says that success is not an accident. Financial success is the result of doing certain, specific things over and over again until you achieve the financial independence that you desire.

Nature is neutral. The natural world, the marketplace, or our society does not care who you are or what you are. The Law of Cause and Effect says that if you do what other successful people do, you will eventually get the results that other successful people get.

And if you don't, you won't. This law says that when you learn the success secrets of self-made millionaires and apply them in your own life, you will experience results and rewards far beyond anything you have accomplished up until now.

Here is an important point for you to remember. **Nobody is better than you and nobody is smarter than you.** Let me repeat that. **Nobody is better than you and nobody is smarter than you.** Get those thoughts out of your mind. One of the primary reasons for selling yourself short, for underachievement and lack of financial success, is the conviction that people who are *doing* better than you are better than you. This is simply not the case.

The fact is that most self-made millionaires are ordinary people with average educations working at average jobs and living in average neighborhoods in average houses driving average cars. But they have found out what other financially successful people do and they have done those same things over and over again until they achieved the same results. It is no miracle and it is no accident. And when you think the same thoughts and do the same things that self-made millionaires do, you will begin to get the same results and benefits they do. It is simply a matter of cause and effect.

There are 21 success secrets of self-made millionaires. Each of these is indispensable to your becoming financially independent. The failure to apply any one of these principles can, by itself, undermine and even destroy your chances for health, happiness, and great prosperity.

The good news is that you can learn every one of these principles by practice and repetition, over and over again, until they become as natural to you as breathing in and breathing out. Just as you learned to ride a bicycle or drive a car, you can learn the success secrets of self-made millionaires and apply them in your life. And there are no limits except the limits you place on yourself by your own thinking. Now, let us begin.

Dream Big Dreams

Dream big dreams; only big dreams
have the power to move men's souls.

—MARCUS AURELIUS

THE FIRST SECRET of self-made millionaires is simple: **Dream Big Dreams!** Allow yourself to dream. Allow yourself to imagine and fantasize about the kind of life you would like to live. Think about the amount of money you would like to earn and have in your bank account.

All great men and women begin with a dream of something wonderful and different from what they have today. You know the song that says "You have to have a dream if you want to make a dream come true." It's true for you and for everyone else, as well.

Imagine that you have no limitations on what you can be, have, or do in life. Just for the moment, imagine that you have all the time, all the money, all the education, all the experience, all the friends, all the contacts, all the resources, and everything else you need to achieve anything you want in life. If your potential were completely unlimited, what kind of a life would you want to create for yourself and your family?

Practice "back from the future" thinking. This is a powerful technique practiced continually by high-performing men and women. This way of thinking has an amazing effect on your mind and on your behavior. Here is how it works: Project yourself forward five years. Imagine that five years have passed and that your life is now perfect in every respect. What does it look like? What are you doing? Where are you working? How much money are you earning? How much do you have in the bank? What kind of a lifestyle do you have?

Create a vision for yourself for the long-term future. The more clear your vision of health, happiness, and prosperity, the faster you move toward it and the faster it moves toward you. When you create a clear mental picture of where you are going in life, you become more positive, more motivated, and more determined to make it a reality. You trigger your natural creativity and come up with idea after idea to help make your vision come true.

You always tend to move in the direction of your dominant dreams, images, and visions. The very act of allowing yourself to dream big dreams actually raises your self-esteem and causes you to like and respect yourself more. It improves your self-concept and increases your level of self-confidence. It increases your personal level of self-respect and happiness. There is something about dreams and visions that is exciting and that stimulates you to do and be better than you ever have before.

Here is a great question for you to ask and answer, over and over again: **What one thing would I dare to dream if I knew I could not fail?**

If you were absolutely guaranteed of success in any one goal in life, large or small, short-term or long-term, what would it be? What one great goal would you dare to dream if you knew you could not fail?

Whatever it is, write it down and begin imagining that you have achieved this one great goal already. Then, look back to where you are today. What would you have done to get where you want to go? What steps would you have taken? What would you have changed in your life? What would you have started up or abandoned? Who would you be with? Who would you no longer be with? If your life were perfect in every respect, what would it look like? Whatever it is that you would do differently, take the first step today.

Dreaming big dreams is the starting point of achieving your goal of financial independence. The number one reason that people never succeed financially is because it never occurs to them that they can do it. As a result, they never try. They never get started. They continue to go around in financial circles, spending everything they earn and a little bit more besides. But when you begin to dream big dreams about financial success, you begin to change the way you see yourself and your life. You begin to do different things, bit by bit, gradually, until the whole direction of your life changes for the better. Dreaming big dreams is the starting point of financial success and of becoming a self-made millionaire.

ACTION EXERCISE

Make a list of everything you would do or attempt if you were absolutely guaranteed of success. Then decide upon one specific action and do it immediately.

SUCCESS

2

SECRET

Develop a Clear Sense of Direction

A person with a clear purpose will make
progress on even the roughest road.
A person with no purpose will make no
progress on even the smoothest road.

—THOMAS CARLYLE

TAKE YOUR DREAMS out of the air and crystallize them
into clear, specific written goals. Perhaps the greatest
discovery in human history is that **"You become what
you think about most of the time."** The two factors
that, more than anything else, determine what happens to you in life are *what* you think about and *how*
you think about it most of the time.

Successful people think about their *goals* most of the time. As a result, they are continually moving toward their goals, and their goals are continually moving toward them. Whatever you think about most of the time grows and increases in your life. If you are thinking about, talking about, and visualizing your goals, you tend to accomplish far, far more than the average person, who is usually thinking and talking about his or her worries and problems most of the time.

Here is a simple seven-step formula for setting and achieving goals that you can use to become a millionaire:

First, decide exactly what you want in each area of your life, especially in your financial life. Most people never do this.

Second, write down your goals clearly and specifically. Something amazing happens between your head and your hand when you put your goals in writing.

Third, set a deadline for each goal. Set subdeadlines if a goal is big enough. Give yourself a target to aim at.

Fourth, make a list of everything you can think of that you will have to do to achieve each goal. As you think of new ideas, add them to your list until it is complete.

Fifth, organize your list into a plan of action. Determine what you are going to do first and what you will do later. Decide what is more important and what is less important.

Sixth, take action on your plan immediately. It is amazing how many splendid goals and plans are never realized because of procrastination and delay.

Seventh, and perhaps most important, do something every day that moves you at least one step closer to your most important goal. This commitment to daily action will make you a big success in anything you decide to accomplish.

Here is an exercise for you. Take a sheet of paper and write the word "Goals" at the top of the page with today's date. Then, make a list of 10 goals that you would like to achieve over the next 12 months. Write your goals in the present tense, as though a year has passed and you have already achieved them. Begin each goal with the word "I" to make it personal to you.

By making out a list of 10 goals for yourself for the next year, you will move yourself into an exclusive group consisting of only 3 percent of adults in our society. The sad fact is that 97 percent of adults have never made a list of goals in their entire lives.

Once you have your list of 10 goals, go over the list and ask this key question: Which *one* goal on this list, if I were to achieve it, would have the greatest positive impact on my life?

Whatever your answer to that question, circle that goal and make that your number one, most important goal for the future. Set a deadline, make a plan, take action on your plan, and do something every day that moves you toward that goal.

From now on, think and talk about that goal all the time. Think and talk about how you can achieve that goal. Think and talk about all the different steps that you can take to make that goal a reality. This exercise will stimulate your creativity, increase your energy, and unlock more and more of your potential.

ACTION EXERCISE

Always think on paper. Sit down and begin writing out your goals and creating your plan to achieve them. This exercise alone can make you a self-made millionaire.

See Yourself as Self-Employed

I am the captain of my soul;

I am the master of my fate.

—WILLIAM HENLEY

FROM NOW ON, accept complete, 100 percent responsibility for everything you are and everything you will ever be. Refuse to make excuses or to blame other people for your problems or shortcomings. Stop complaining about things in your life that you are not happy about. Refuse to criticize other people for anything. You are responsible. If there is something in your life that you don't like, it is up to you to change it. You are in charge.

The top 3 percent of Americans see themselves as self-employed, no matter who signs their paychecks. The biggest mistake you can ever make is to think that you work for anyone other than yourself. You are always self-employed. You are always the president of your own personal service corporation, no matter where you might be working at the moment.

When you see yourself as self-employed, you develop an *entrepreneur* mentality, the mentality of highly independent, self-responsible, self-starting individuals. Instead of *waiting* for things to happen, you *make* things happen. You see yourself as the boss of your own life. You see yourself as completely in charge of your physical health, your financial well-being, your career, your relationships, your lifestyle, your home, your car, and every other element of your existence. This is the mind-set of the self-made millionaire.

Self-responsible people are intensely result oriented. They always take high levels of initiative. They volunteer for assignments and are always asking for more responsibility. As a result, they become the most valuable and respected people in their organizations. They continually prepare themselves for positions of higher authority and responsibility in the future. You should do the same.

Here's a question: **If you were president of your company for a day or were completely responsible for results where you work, what one change would you enact immediately?**

Whatever it is, write it down, make a plan, and begin implementing it today. This action alone could change your life.

ACTION EXERCISE

Identify your favorite reasons and excuses for not committing wholeheartedly to your financial goals. Is there anyone or anything in your life that you are blaming for holding you back? Whatever it might be, accept complete responsibility for your life and take action today!

Do What You Love to Do

When you start doing what you really love to do, you'll never work another day in your life.

— BRIAN TRACY

DOING WHAT YOU love to do is one of the great secrets of financial success. One of your primary responsibilities in life is to find out what you really enjoy doing, what you have a natural talent for, and then to throw your whole heart into doing that particular work very, very well.

Self-made millionaires are those who have found a field where their natural strengths and abilities are exactly what is required to do the job and achieve the results desired. Most self-made millionaires say that they *"never worked a day in their life."* You must find a field in which you can be totally absorbed—a job or area of endeavor that completely fascinates you, that holds your attention, that is a natural expression of your special talents and abilities.

When you are doing what you love to do, you seem to have a continuous flow of excitement, energy, and ideas to do what you do even better. Here is a question for you: **If you won a million dollars, tax free, tomorrow, would you continue to do what you are currently doing?**

This is a great question. It simply asks you what you would do if you had all the time and money you needed and you were free to choose your occupation. Self-made millionaires, if they won a million dollars cash, would continue doing what they are doing. They would only do it differently or better or at a higher level. But they love their work so much that they wouldn't even think of leaving it or retiring.

Perhaps the greatest responsibility of adult life, when you are surrounded by so many different choices of occupation and career, is for you to find out what you really love doing and then dedicate yourself to that field. And no one else can do this for you.

ACTION EXERCISE

Identify the type of work that you enjoy the most. What activities have been most responsible for your success in life to date? If you could do any job at all and be successful at it, what would you choose? Set it as a goal, make a plan, and begin moving in that direction today.

Commit to Excellence

The quality of your life will be

determined by the depth of your

commitment to excellence, no matter

what your chosen field.

—Vince Lombardi

Resolve today to be the very best at what you do. Set a goal for yourself to join the top 10 percent of your field, whatever it is. This decision, to become very, very good at what you do, can be the turning point in your life. Virtually all successful people are recognized as being extremely competent in their chosen fields.

Remember that no one is better than you, and no one is smarter than you. And everyone who is in the top 10 percent today started off in the bottom 10 percent. Everyone who is doing well was once doing poorly. Everyone who is at the top of his or her field was at one time in another field altogether. And what countless others have done, you can do as well.

Here is a great rule for success: *Your life only gets better when you get better.* And since there is no limit to how much better you can become, there is no limit to how much better you can make your life.

Your decision to become excellent at what you do, to join the top 10 percent in your field, is the turning point in your life. It is the key to great success. It is also the foundation of high levels of self-esteem, self-respect, and personal pride. When you are really good at what you do, you feel wonderful about yourself. Being excellent affects your whole personality and all your relationships with other people. You feel happy and proud when you know you are at the top of your field.

Here is one of the most important questions you will ever ask and answer, for the rest of your career: **What one skill, if I developed and did it in an excellent fashion, would have the greatest positive impact on my life?**

You cannot become good at everything right away, but you can identify the one skill that can help you the most and then throw your whole heart into developing that skill. Set it as a goal. Write it down. Set a deadline. Make a plan. And work on becoming better in that area every single day. You will be absolutely amazed at the difference this commitment to excellence will make in your life. This commitment alone can make you a self-made millionaire in the course of your career.

◆

ACTION EXERCISE

Identify your key result areas in your current job. What are the parts of your work that you must absolutely, positively perform in an excellent fashion to move to the top of your field? Where are you strong and where are you weak? Make a plan today to get better in the one skill area where improvement can help you the most.

SUCCESS

6

SECRET

Work Longer and Harder

The harder I work, the luckier I get.

—JAMES THURBER

ALL SELF-MADE millionaires work hard, hard, hard. They start earlier, they work harder, and they stay later. They develop a reputation for being amongst the hardest working people in their fields. And everybody knows it.

Practice the "40 Plus" formula. This formula says that you work 40 hours per week for survival; everything over 40 hours is for success. If you work only 40 hours (and the average workweek today is closer to 35 hours), all you will ever do is survive. You will never get ahead. You will never be a big financial success. You will never be highly respected and esteemed by your colleagues. You will always be mediocre working the basic 40-hour week.

22

But every hour over 40 hours is an investment in your future. In fact, you can tell with tremendous accuracy where you are going to be in five years by looking at how many hours over 40 you put in every week. There is just no substitute for long days and hard work.

Self-made millionaires in America work an average of 59 hours per week. Many of them work 70 or 80 hours, especially at the start of their careers. They work an average of six days per week, rather than five, and work longer days as well. If you want to call a self-made millionaire, phone the office before normal working hours and after normal working hours. The self-made millionaire is there when the staff, the "nine-to-fivers," arrive and is still there when they leave.

And here's the key: **Work all the time you work.** When you work, don't waste time. When you get in early, put your head down and get started immediately. When people want to talk to you, excuse yourself and say, "I have to get back to work!"

Do not drop off your dry cleaning, phone your friends, socialize with your coworkers, or read the newspaper. Work all the time you work. Resolve today to develop the reputation for being the hardest working person in your company. This will bring you to the attention of people who can help you faster than almost anything else you can do.

◆

ACTION EXERCISE

Make a plan today to increase the number of hours you work each day. Resolve to get to the office one hour earlier and get a head start on the day. Work at lunchtime when others are gone. Stay one hour later to get caught up. This strategy alone will double your output while adding only two hours to your day.

Dedicate Yourself to Lifelong Learning

Continuous learning is the minimum requirement for success in any field.

—DENIS WAITLEY

YOU HAVE A virtually unlimited capacity to learn and improve in your chosen field. You have more brains, ability, and intelligence than you could ever use if you were to work on developing yourself for the rest of your life. You are smarter than you can even imagine. There is no obstacle that you cannot overcome, no problem you cannot solve, and no goal you cannot achieve by applying the power of your mind to your situation.

But your mind is like a muscle. It develops only with use. Just as you have to strain your physical muscles to build them, you have to work your mental muscles to build your mind as well. The good news is that the more you learn, the more you can learn. Just like the more you play a sport, the better you get at the sport. The more you dedicate yourself to lifelong learning, the easier it is for you to learn even more.

Leaders are learners. Continuous learning is the key to the 21st century. Lifelong learning is the minimum requirement for success in your field or in any field. Make a decision today that you are going to become a student of your craft and that you are going to continue learning and becoming better for the rest of your life.

There are three keys to lifelong learning. The first key is to read in your field for at least 30 to 60 minutes each day. **Reading is to the mind as exercise is to the body.** Reading for an hour each day will translate into about one book per week. One book per week will translate into 50 books per year. Fifty books per year will translate into 500 books over the next 10 years.

Since the average adult reads less than one book per year, when you begin reading one hour per day, one book per week, this alone will give you an incredible edge in your field. You will become one of the smartest, most competent, and highest paid people in your profession by simply reading one hour each day.

The second key to lifelong learning is to listen to audio programs in your car as you drive from place to place. The average person sits behind the wheel in his or her car 500 to 1,000 hours per year. This is the equivalent of 12 to 24 forty-hour weeks, or as much as three to six months of working time that you spend in your car. This is the equivalent of one to two full-time semesters at a university.

Turn your car into a *learning machine,* into a university on wheels. Never let your car motor be running without an educational audio program playing. Many people have become millionaires through the miracle of audio learning. This is why audio learning is often called the greatest breakthrough in education since the invention of the printing press.

A third key to lifelong learning is to attend every course and seminar you can possibly find that can help you to be better in your field. The combination of books, audio programs, and seminars will enable you to save hundreds of hours and thousands of dollars, and many years of hard work, in achieving the level of financial success that you desire.

Make a decision today to become a lifelong learner. You will be amazed at the effect that it has in your career. Lifelong learning can be a major factor in your becoming a self-made millionaire.

◆

ACTION EXERCISE

Select a subject that can really help you to be more productive and effective in your field. Set a goal to master this subject. Make it a "do-it-to-yourself" project. Then, read on this subject every day. Listen to audio programs on the subject. Attend courses on the subject. Work on this project as if your future depends on it, because it does!

Pay Yourself First

A part of all you earn is yours to keep,
and if you cannot save money, the
seeds of greatness are not in you.

—W. Clement Stone

Resolve today that you are going to save and invest at least 10 percent of your income throughout your working life. Take 10 percent of your income off the top of your paycheck each time you receive one and put it into a special account for financial accumulation. The fact is that if you save just $100 per month throughout your working lifetime and you invest that money in an average mutual fund that grows at 10 percent per annum, you will be worth more than one million dollars by the time you retire. This means that anyone, even a person earning minimum wage, if he or she starts early enough and saves long enough, can become a millionaire over the course of his or her working lifetime.

Developing the lifelong habit of saving and invest-
ing your money is not easy. It requires tremendous
determination and willpower. You have to set it as a
goal, write it down, make a plan, and work on it all the
time. But once this practice locks in and becomes automatic, your financial success is virtually assured.

Practice frugality, frugality, frugality in all things.
Be very careful with every penny. Question every expenditure. Delay or defer every important buying decision for at least a week, if not a month. The longer
you put off making a buying decision, the better your
decision will be and the better price you will get at
that time.

A major reason that people retire poor is because
of impulse buying. They see something they like and
they buy it with very little thought. They become vic-
tims of what is called "Parkinson's Law," which says
that "expenses rise to meet income." This means that
no matter how much you earn, you tend to spend that
much and a little bit more besides. You never get
ahead and you never get out of debt.

But you don't have to be a victim of Parkinson's
Law. If you cannot save 10 percent of your income,
start today by saving 1 percent of your income in a
special savings and investment account. Put it away at
the beginning of each month, even before you begin
paying down your debts. Live on the other 99 percent
of your income. As you become comfortable living on

99 percent, raise your savings level to 2 percent of your income, then 3 percent and 4 percent, and so on.

Within one year, you will be saving 10 percent and maybe even 15 percent or 20 percent of your income and living comfortably on the balance. At the same time, your savings and investment account will start to grow. You will become more careful about your expenditures, and your debts will begin to be paid off. Within a year or two, your entire financial life will be under your control and you will be on your way to becoming a self-made millionaire. This process has worked for everyone who has ever tried it. Try it and see for yourself.

ACTION EXERCISE

Open a special account for financial accumulation today. Make a deposit in this account, no matter how small. Then, look for every opportunity to add to this account. Begin to study money so that you understand how to make it grow. Read books and magazines by experts on the subject. Never stop saving, learning, and growing until you become financially independent.

Learn Every Detail of Your Business

If you become very good at what you do, there is nothing that can stop you from getting paid more and promoted faster.

—DAN KENNEDY

THE MARKET PAYS excellent rewards for excellent performance. It pays average rewards for average performance and below-average rewards, failure, and frustration for below-average performance. Your goal should be to become an expert in your chosen field by learning every single detail about how to do your work better and better.

Read all the magazines in your field. Read and study the latest books. Attend courses and seminars given by experts in your field. Join your industry or trade association, attend every meeting, and get involved with the other top people in your field.

The Law of Integrative Complexity says that the individual who can integrate and use the greatest amount of information in any field soon rises to the top of that field.

If you are in sales, become an aggressive, lifelong student of the selling process. The top 20 percent of salespeople earn, on average, 16 times the amount earned by the bottom 80 percent of salespeople. The top 10 percent of salespeople earn even more.

If you are in management, resolve to become an outstanding professional manager. If you are starting and building your own business, study entrepreneurial strategies and tactics and try out new ideas every single day.

Set a goal for yourself to become the very best in your business or profession. One small detail, insight, or idea can be the turning point in your career. Never stop looking for it.

ACTION EXERCISE

Identify the trends in your business. What are the core competencies or key skills that you will need to lead your field in the future? Make a plan today to develop those skills and then work on them every day.

Dedicate Yourself to Serving Others

You can get everything you want

in life if you just help enough

other people get what they want.

—Zig Ziglar

YOUR REWARDS IN life will always be in direct proportion to your service to other people. All self-made millionaires have an obsession with customer service. They think about their customers all the time. They are continually looking for new and better ways to serve their customers better than anyone else.

Keep asking yourself these questions, What do my customers really want? What do my customers really need? What do my customers consider value? What can I give my customers better than anyone else? Why are my customers buying from others today, and what would I have to offer them to get them to buy from me?

Your success in life will be in direct proportion to what you do after you do what you are expected to do. Always look for opportunities to do more than you are paid for. Always seek ways to go the extra mile for your customers. Remember, there are never any traffic jams on the extra mile.

Your customers are those people who you depend on for your success in your work. This means that your boss and coworkers are customers as well as the people who buy your products or services. Your customers are also those people who depend on you for their success or satisfaction.

Here is the question that you need to ask and answer, every single day: **What can I do to increase the value of my service to my customers today?**

Look for ways to add value to what you do and to the people who depend on you every single day. One small improvement in the way you serve your customers can be a major reason for your financial success. Never stop looking for those little ways to serve your customers better.

Today, customers value speed more than they've ever valued it before. Whenever a customer asks for anything, you should say, "Sure, right away!" These are the sweetest words your customers can hear.

◆

ACTION EXERCISE

Identify your most important customers, both inside and outside your company. Who are the people you most depend upon? Who are the people who most depend upon you? What could you do, starting today, to take better care of them?

Be Absolutely Honest with Yourself and Others

Thought is the original source of all wealth, all success, all material gain, all great discoveries and inventions, and all achievement.

—CLAUDE M. BRISTOL

PERHAPS THE MOST valued and respected quality you can develop is a reputation for absolute integrity. Be perfectly honest in everything you do and in every transaction and activity. Never compromise your integrity. Remember that your word is your bond and your honor is everything when it comes to business.

All successful business is based on trust. Your success in becoming a self-made millionaire will be determined solely by the number of people who trust you and who are willing to work for you, give you credit, lend you money, buy your products and services, and help you during difficult times. Your character is the most important asset that you develop in your entire life, and your character is based on the amount of integrity that you practice.

The first key to integrity is to be true to yourself, in all things. Be true to the very best that is in you. Being true to yourself means doing what you do in an excellent fashion. Integrity is demonstrated internally by personal honesty and externally by quality work.

The second key to integrity is to be true to the other people in your life. Live in truth with everyone. Never do or say anything that you do not believe to be right and good and honest. Refuse to compromise your integrity for anything. Always live up to the very highest standard that you know.

Here is a question for you to ask and answer on a regular basis: **What kind of a world would my world be if everyone in it was just like me?**

This question forces you to set high standards for yourself and keep raising the bar. Act as though your every word and action were to become a universal law. Carry yourself as though everyone were watching you and patterning his or her behavior after yours. And when in doubt, always do the right thing, whatever it is and whatever it costs.

ACTION EXERCISE

Almost every problem in your life can be resolved by a return to your values. What are they? What do you believe in and stand for? Whenever you experience stress of any kind, it usually means that you are compromising one of your values. Whatever it is, resolve this very minute to be true to what you really believe to be important in your life.

Determine Your Highest Priorities and Concentrate on Them Single-Mindedly

"A double minded man is unstable in all his ways." Do what comes to your hand to do.

—Brian Tracy

When you develop the habit of setting priorities and concentrating single-mindedly, you will be able to accomplish virtually anything you want in life. This core strategy has been the primary reason for high income, wealth creation, and financial independence for thousands and even millions of people.

Your ability to determine your highest priority and then to work on that high priority until it is completed is the primary test and measure of your willpower, self-discipline, and personal character. It is the hardest habit to develop but also the most important if you want to be a big success.

Here is the formula. Make a list of everything you have to do before you begin working toward any goal. Set priorities on that list by asking yourself four questions, over and over.

Question number one is, **What are my highest value activities?** What do you do that is more valuable than anything else to your work and your business?

Question number two is, **Why am I on the payroll?** What exactly have you been hired to accomplish? Focus on results, not activities.

Question number three is, **What can I and only I do that, if done well, will make a real difference?** This is a particular task that only you can do. If you don't do it, it won't get done. But if you do do it and you do it well, it can make a significant difference in your business or your personal life. What is that task?

Question number four is, **What is the most valuable use of my time right now?** There is only one answer to this question at any time. Your ability to determine the single most valuable use of your time and then to start on that task is the key to high productivity and financial success.

Finally, commit to working single-mindedly on one task, the most important task, and staying at it until it is 100 percent complete. Persevere without diversion or distraction. Push yourself to keep working at the job until it is done.

The good news is that by continually setting priorities and concentrating on your highest value tasks, you will soon develop the habit of high performance. This habit will then become automatic and will virtually guarantee you great success in life. This one habit alone can make you a self-made millionaire.

ACTION EXERCISE

Identify the most important thing that you can do right now to achieve your most important goal and then discipline yourself to do that, and only that, until it is 100 percent complete. Your ability to do this, and this alone, can change your whole life.

Develop a Reputation for Speed and Dependability

Do your work; not just your work

and no more, but a little bit more for

the lavishings sake, that little more

which is worth more than all the rest.

—DEAN BRIGGS

TIME IS THE currency of the 21st century. Everyone today is in a tremendous hurry. Customers who did not even know that they wanted a product or service now want it yesterday. People are less and less patient for anything. Loyal customers will change suppliers overnight if someone else can serve them faster than the people they are already dealing with. Instant gratification is no longer fast enough.

Your job is to develop a reputation for speed. Develop a "sense of urgency." Develop a bias for action. Move fast on opportunities. Move fast when people want or need something. Move quickly when you see something that needs to be done.

When your boss or your customers ask you to do something, drop everything else and do it so fast that they are amazed. You have heard it said that "Whenever you want to get something done, give it to a busy person." People who have a reputation for moving quickly attract more opportunities and possibilities to them. They get more chances to do more and more things faster than other people who just do a job when they get around to it.

When you can combine your ability to select your highest priority task with the commitment to getting it done quickly and well, you will find yourself moving to the front. More doors and opportunities will open for you than you can even imagine today.

ACTION EXERCISE

Select just one key task that you have been procrastinating on starting, or bringing to completion, and resolve to take action on it immediately. Keep repeating to yourself these magic motivating words: "Do it now! Do it now! Do it now!"

Be Prepared to Climb from Peak to Peak

Winning is not a sometime thing;

it's an all the time thing.

—VINCE LOMBARDI

JUST AS A mountain climber who has reached one peak must go down into the valley before climbing to another peak, your life and career will be a series of ups and downs. As you've heard, "Life is a process of two steps forward and one step back."

All business life is made up of cycles and trends. There are up cycles and down cycles. Often, trends in business can lead to a complete change in the industry. We see this today with the Internet and the expansion of technology in all directions, which are changing many of our fixed ideas and beliefs about the way business is done.

Develop a long-time perspective. Take the long view in everything you do. Plan two, three, four, and five years into the future and don't allow yourself to get onto an emotional roller coaster with the short-term ups and downs of daily life.

Keep reminding yourself that everything in your life moves in cycles and trends. Be calm, confident, and relaxed with short-term fluctuations in your fortune. When you have clear goals and plans that you are working on every day, the general trend line of your life will tend to be onward and upward over the years.

ACTION EXERCISE

Identify the key cycles and trends in your business. Where is the market going? What is changing and how will you have to adapt to these changes? What steps should you be taking today to be ready to take advantage of the new world of tomorrow? Whatever your answer, take those steps now!

Practice Self-Discipline in All Things

Self-discipline is the ability to

make yourself do what you should do,

when you should do it,

whether you feel like it or not.

—ELBERT HUBBARD

SELF-DISCIPLINE IS the most important single quality for success in life and in becoming a self-made millionaire. If you can discipline yourself to do what you should do, when you should do it, whether you feel like it or not, your success is virtually guaranteed.

The key to becoming a self-made millionaire is having a long-time perspective combined with an ability to delay gratification in the short term. It is your ability to set a long-term goal of becoming financially independent and then to discipline yourself, every single day and with every single expenditure, to do only those things that will guarantee that you ultimately achieve your long-term goal.

Self-discipline requires self-mastery, self-control, self-responsibility, and self-direction. The difference between successful people and failures is that successful people make a habit of doing the things that failures do not like to do. And what are those things? The things that failures don't like to do are the same things that successful people don't like to do either. But successful people do them anyway because they realize that this is the price they must pay for the success they desire.

Successful people are more concerned with pleasing *results*. Failures are more concerned with pleasing *methods*. Successful people take actions that are goal achieving. Unsuccessful people take actions that are tension relieving. Successful people do the things that are hard and necessary and important. Unsuccessful people, on the other hand, prefer to do the things that are fun and easy and that give them immediate enjoyment.

The good news is that every act of self-discipline strengthens your other disciplines as well. Every time you practice self-discipline, your self-esteem goes up. You like and respect yourself even more. And the more you practice discipline in small things, the more capable you become of the great disciplines required for the great opportunities, experiences, and challenges of life.

Remember that everything in life is a *test*. Every day, every hour, and sometimes every minute, you are taking a test—of self-mastery, self-control, and self-discipline. The test is to see whether you can make yourself do the things that are most important and stay with them until they are complete. The test is whether you can keep your mind on what you want and where you are going rather than thinking and talking about things you don't want or problems you have had in the past. When you pass the test, you move onward and upward to the next "grade." And as long as you keep passing the tests, you keep moving onward and upward in your life. Success requires tons of discipline. As Jim Rohn says, "Discipline weighs ounces; failure weighs tons."

ACTION EXERCISE

Change one thing at a time. Identify one area of your life where lack of discipline is interfering with your success. Decide today to develop discipline in that area. Launch strongly. Tell others about your decision. Never allow exceptions until the new habit is firmly entrenched. This decision alone could change your life.

Unlock Your Inborn Creativity

Imagination is more important

than facts.

—ALBERT EINSTEIN

HERE IS SOME more good news. You are a *potential* genius. You are smarter than you have ever imagined. You have more raw brainpower and creative ability than you have ever used up to now.

Your brain has 10 billion cells, each of which is connected to as many as 20,000 other cells by a complex network of neurons and dendrites. This means that the possible combinations and permutations of cells in your brain are greater than the number of molecules in the known universe. Your ability to develop ideas to help you succeed is unlimited. This means that your ability to succeed is unlimited as well.

Your creativity is stimulated by three factors: first, intensely desired goals; second, pressing problems; and third, focused questions. The more you focus your mind on achieving your goals, solving your problems, or answering the tough questions about your business and personal life, the smarter you become and the better your mind works for you in the future.

Your brain, your creativity, is like a muscle. The more you use it, the stronger and more resilient it becomes. You can actually increase your intelligence and your IQ by disciplining yourself to think creatively all day long. And remember, creativity is just another word for *"improvement."* Every time you come up with an idea to improve some part of your work, to find newer, better, faster, cheaper, or easier ways to accomplish a result, you are functioning at the highest level of creativity.

Just as you develop your muscles by straining them with physical training, you develop your mental muscles by straining them as well. Here is an exercise for you to develop your brainpower and unlock your inner genius.

Take a clean sheet of paper and write your most important goal or most pressing problem at the top in the form of a question. For example, you could write, "How can I double my income over the next 24 to 36 months?"

Now, discipline yourself to write at least 20 different answers to your question. Select one of your answers and take action on it immediately. You will be amazed at the results.

◆

ACTION EXERCISE

Write down your most pressing prob- lem or your most intensely desired goal. Then, imagine that this problem was solved perfectly or this goal was achieved in an ideal way. What would the solution or achievement look like? What could you do immediately to bring about this result? Remember, ac- tion is everything!

Get around the Right People

You will be the same person in five years except for the people you meet and the books you read.

—CHARLIE JONES

FULLY 85 PERCENT of your success and happiness in life is going to be determined by the quality of the relationships that you develop in your personal and your business activities. The more people you know and who know you in a positive way, the more successful you will be and the faster you will move ahead.

At virtually every turning point in your life, someone is standing there to either help you or hinder you. Successful people make a habit of building and maintaining a network of high-quality relationships throughout their lives, and as a result, they accomplish vastly more than the person who goes home and watches television each night.

Everything involves relationships. Virtually all of your problems in life will come as the result of your entering into wrong relationships with the wrong people. Virtually all of your great successes in life will be accompanied by great relationships with good people who help you and whom you help in return.

More than 90 percent of your success will be determined by your "reference group." Your reference group is defined as the people with whom you habitually identify and pass the time.

You are like a chameleon in that you take on the attitudes, behaviors, values, and beliefs of the people with whom you associate most of the time. If you want to be a successful person, associate with positive people. Associate with people who are optimistic and happy and who have goals and who are moving forward in their lives. At the same time, get away from negative, critical, complaining people. If you want to fly with the eagles, you cannot scratch with the turkeys.

Self-made millionaires network continually. They join their industry and trade associations, attend every meeting, and get involved in the groups' activities. They introduce themselves to people in business and social settings, hand out their business cards, and tell others what they do.

And here is one of the best strategies of all. Whenever you meet new people, ask them to tell you about their businesses and, especially, to tell you what you would need to know to send clients or customers to them.

Then, as soon as possible, see if you can send some business their way. Be a "go-giver" rather than a go-getter. Always look for ways to put in before you start thinking of ways to take out. The very best way to network and build your relationships is to constantly look for ways to help other people achieve their own goals. The more you give of yourself without expecting something in return, the more rewards will come back to you from the most unexpected sources.

ACTION EXERCISE

Identify the most important people in your life, both present and future. What could you do to help them in their lives and work so that they would be open to helping you? Identify the people you should get to know. What could you do to help them in advance of your needing anything in return? Remember, first you sow and then you reap.

Take Excellent Care of Your Physical Health

The key to happiness is a sound mind in a sound body.

—THEODORE ROOSEVELT

WE ARE LIVING at the most wonderful time in human history in terms of longevity and physical fitness. You can live longer and live better today than has ever before been possible. You should aim to live to be 80 or 90 or even 100 years old, in excellent health, and you can do it if you decide to.

First, set a goal to live to be at least 80 years old. Then, look at your current health habits and ask yourself whether or not the way you are living today is going to get you to the age of 80 in great shape.

There are three keys to living a long, happy, healthy life. The first is proper weight. Set a goal to get your weight under control and then remain lean and fit for the rest of your life. There is a five-word formula for weight loss and physical fitness. It is simply this: "Eat less and exercise more."

The second key is proper diet, and the key to a proper diet is to eat better foods and fewer of them. Eat more lean proteins, fruits, and vegetables. Eliminate desserts, soft drinks, candy, and anything else containing sugar from your life. Stop consuming extra salt and stop eating white flour products. Eat smaller portions and eat four or five times a day rather than three large meals.

When you can take complete control of your eating habits, you will find it easier to take control of your habits in other parts of your life as well.

The third key to long life is proper exercise. This requires that you engage in vigorous physical activity approximately 200 minutes per week or an average of 30 minutes per day. You can get all the exercise you need by going for a brisk 30-to-60-minute walk three to five days per week. If you are really serious, you should join a health club or get some fitness equipment for your house and work out even more vigorously.

The key to excellent physical health and long life is to set clear, specific goals for your levels of health and fitness. You must make a plan and then follow your plan every day. This commitment to health requires tremendous self-mastery, self-control, and self-discipline, but the payoff can be extraordinary.

If your financial goal is to achieve a net worth in excess of one million dollars, your health goal should be to live as long as possible so that you can enjoy a wonderful lifestyle with your money.

ACTION EXERCISE

Identify one health habit that you need to develop to enjoy higher levels of health and energy. Perhaps it is eliminating desserts altogether. Then, set this as a personal challenge and resolve to discipline yourself until your new health habit is firmly entrenched.

Be Decisive and Action Oriented

Take arms against a sea of troubles,

and in so doing, end them.

—WILLIAM SHAKESPEARE

ONE OF THE qualities of self-made millionaires is that they think carefully and then make decisions quickly. They discipline themselves to take action and to carry out the decisions they have made. They move fast and they get quick feedback from their actions. If they find they have made a mistake, they quickly self-correct and try something else.

The key to triumph is for you to *try.* Successful people are decisive and they try far more things than other people do. According to the Law of Probabilities, if you try far more different ways to be successful, the odds are that you will eventually find the right way for you at the right time.

Unsuccessful people are indecisive. They know that they should do or stop doing certain things, but they do not have the character or the willpower to make firm decisions. As a result, they drift through life, never happy, fulfilled, or successful. They never become wealthy or achieve financial independence. They settle for far less than is possible for them.

When you become decisive and action oriented, you shift your entire life into high gear. You get far more done in a day than other people. You move ahead far faster than the people around you. You actually tap into a higher source of energy, enthusiasm, and motivation that fills you full of joy and exhilaration. This positive energy then propels you forward even faster toward your goals.

◆

ACTION EXERCISE

Ask yourself, What one action, if I did it immediately, could have the greatest positive impact on my results? *Whatever your answer to that question, just do it!*

Never Allow Failure to Be an Option

There is nothing to fear but fear itself.

—FRANKLIN D. ROOSEVELT

THE FEAR OF failure is the greatest single obstacle to success in adult life. Note that it is not failure itself. Failure makes you stronger and more resilient and more determined. It is the *fear* of failure or the *anticipation* of failure that can paralyze your thoughts and your activities and hold you back from even trying to do the things that you need to do to be a big success.

A young journalist once asked Thomas J. Watson Sr., the founder of IBM, how he could be more successful faster. Watson replied with these wonderful words: *"If you want to be successful faster, you must double your rate of failure. Success lies on the far side of failure."*

66

Dare to go forward. Self-made millionaires are not gamblers, but they are always willing to take calculated risks in the direction of their goals to achieve greater rewards. In fact, your attitude toward risk taking is probably the most important indicator of your readiness to become wealthy.

Whenever you are faced with a risky situation, ask yourself this question, *What is the worst possible thing that could happen if I go ahead?* Then, as J. Paul Getty, the self-made oil billionaire, said, you should make sure that, whatever it is, it doesn't happen.

The fact is that everyone is afraid of failure. Everyone is afraid of loss and poverty. Everyone is afraid of making a mistake and being set back. But self-made millionaires are those who consciously and deliberately face this fear and take action anyway. Ralph Waldo Emerson wrote, **"Make a habit throughout your life of doing the things you fear. If you do the thing you fear, the death of fear is certain."**

When you act boldly, unseen forces will come to your aid. And every act of courage increases your courage and capacity for courage in the future. Whenever you take action in a forward direction with no guarantees of success, your fears diminish and your courage and self-confidence increase. You eventually reach the point where you are not afraid of anything.

Perhaps the best line from the movie *Apollo 13* came from Eugene Krantz, head of mission control at NASA. When the people around him were starting to think about the possibility of losing the spacecraft and the astronauts, he pulled them all together by announcing in a loud voice, *"Failure is not an option!"*

Your job is to commit yourself to becoming a self-made millionaire. Your job is to set specific goals for yourself, write them down, and work toward them every day. And especially, you must continue to remind yourself, in the face of all the problems and difficulties that you will experience, that **"Failure is not an option!"** This is the attitude that, more than anything else, will guarantee your long-term success.

ACTION EXERCISE

Identify one major fear in your life— for example, failure, criticism, or disapproval—and resolve to act as if the fear did not exist. Imagine that you were guaranteed success if you would only take action in the direction of your goals and dreams. Then, just do it!

Pass the "Persistence Test"

Nothing can take the place of persistence.
Talent will not; nothing is more common
than unsuccessful men with talent.
Genius will not; unrewarded genius is
almost a proverb. Education will not;
the world is full of educated derelicts.
Persistence and determination alone
are omnipotent.

—CALVIN COOLIDGE

PERSISTENCE IS THE iron quality of character. Persistence is to the character of man as carbon is to steel. It is the absolutely indispensable quality that goes hand in hand with all great success in life.

And here is one of the great secrets of persistence and success: Program your subconscious mind for persistence well in advance of the setbacks and disappointments that you are going to have on your upward quest toward success. Resolve *in advance* that you will never give up, no matter what happens.

When you are overwhelmed with a problem or difficulty, you do not have enough time to develop the necessary persistence to deal with the setback or disappointment. But if you plan in advance for the inevitable ups and downs of life, when they come, you will be psychologically ready. You will be prepared.

The courage to persist in the face of adversity and disappointment is the one quality that, more than anything, will guarantee your success. Your greatest personal asset can be your willingness to persevere longer than anyone else. In fact, your persistence is a true measure of your belief in yourself and your ability to succeed.

Remember, all of life is a test. For you to have great success, you must pass the *"persistence test."* And this test is often a pop quiz. It can come at any time, usually totally unexpectedly and out of left field. You take the persistence test whenever you are confronted with an unexpected difficulty, disappointment, setback, failure, or crisis in life. This is where you show yourself, and everyone around you, what you are truly made of.

Epictetus, a Greek philosopher, once wrote, "Circumstances do not make the man. They merely reveal him to himself."

The one inevitability in your life is recurring crisis. If you are living a busy life, you will have a crisis every two or three months. In between these unavoidable crises will be a continuous succession of problems and difficulties. And the more goals that you attempt to reach, the bigger your dreams, and the more determined you are to become a self-made millionaire, the more problems and crises you will experience.

The only factor you can control is how you respond to difficulties and setbacks. And the good news is that every time you respond in a positive and constructive manner, you become stronger and better and even more capable of dealing with the next problem or crisis that comes along. Eventually, you will reach a point in life where you become absolutely unstoppable.

You will become like a force of nature. You will be irresistible. You will become the kind of person who never quits, no matter what the difficulty. No matter what obstacle is put in your path, you will find a way to go over it, under it, around it, or through it. You will be like the Energizer Bunny in the television commercials. You will keep going and going and going.

◆

ACTION EXERCISE

What is the most difficult situation you are facing in your life today? Whatever it is, imagine that it has been sent to you at this time to teach you a valuable lesson that you need to learn to be even more successful in the future. What could that lesson be? From this moment onward, always seek the valuable lesson in every setback or difficulty. You will always find it, and it will help you in your quest to become a self-made millionaire.

Conclusion:
Success Is Predictable

L et me repeat the most important message of this entire book. It is this: "Success is predictable."

Success is not a matter of luck or accident or being in the right place at the right time. Success is as predictable as the sun rising in the east and setting in the west. By practicing the principles that you have just learned, you will move to the front of the line in life. You will have an incredible advantage over people who do not know or who do not practice these techniques and strategies. You will have an advantage that will give you the winning edge for the rest of your life and career.

If you consistently and persistently do the things that other successful people do, nothing in the world can stop you from becoming a big success yourself. You are the architect of your own destiny. You are the master of your own fate. You are behind the steering wheel of your own life. There are no limitations to what you can do, have, or be except the limitations you place on yourself by your own thinking.

Remember, you are as good or better than anyone you will ever meet. You are an outstanding human being. You have talents and abilities far greater than anything you have ever realized or used up to now. You have within you the potential to accomplish wonderful things with your life. Your greatest responsibilities are to dream big dreams, decide exactly what you want, make a plan to achieve it, practice the strategies taught in this book, take action every single day in the direction of your dreams and goals, and resolve to never, never, never give up. When you take these actions, you put yourself on the side of the angels. You become unstoppable and your success becomes inevitable.

About the Author

BRIAN TRACY is a professional speaker, trainer, and consultant and is the chairman of Brian Tracy International, a training and consulting company based in Solana Beach, California. He is also a self-made millionaire.

Brian learned his lessons the hard way. He left high school without graduating and worked as a laborer for several years. He washed dishes, stacked lumber, dug wells, worked in factories, and stacked hay bales on farms and ranches.

In his mid-20s, he became a salesman and began climbing up through the business world. Year by year, studying and applying every idea, method, and technique he could find, he worked his way up to become chief operating officer of a $265-million development company.

In his 30s, he enrolled at the University of Alberta and earned a bachelor of commerce degree, then he earned a master's degree in administration and management from Columbia Pacific University. Over the years, he has worked in 22 different companies and industries. In 1981, he began teaching his success principles in talks and seminars around the country. Today, his books, audio programs, and video seminars have been translated into 20 languages and are used in 38 countries.

Brian has one single focus. He believes that the average (or above-average) person has enormous untapped potential. He believes that you can move ahead far faster toward your goals if you learn and practice the key methods, techniques, and strategies used by other successful people who have gone before you.

Brian has shared his ideas with more than two million people in 23 countries since he began speaking professionally. He has served as a consultant and trainer for more than 500 corporations. He has lived and practiced every principle in this book. He has taken himself and countless thousands of other people from frustration and underachievement to prosperity and success.

Brian Tracy calls himself an "eclectic reader." He considers himself not an academic researcher but a synthesizer of information. Each year he spends hundreds of hours reading a wide variety of newspapers, magazines, books, and other materials. In addition, he listens to many hours of audio programs, attends countless seminars, and watches numerous videotapes on subjects of interest to him. Information gleaned from radio, television, and other media also adds to his knowledge base.

Brian assimilates ideas and information based on his own experience, and that of others, and incorporates them into his own experience. He is the best-selling author of more than a dozen books, including *Maximum Achievement, Advanced Selling Strategies* and *The 100 Absolutely Unbreakable Laws of Business Success.* He has written and produced more than 300 audio and video learning programs that have been translated into 20 languages and are taught in 35 countries.

Brian is happily married and has four children. He lives on a golf course in San Diego. He travels and speaks more than 100 times each year and has business operations in 17 countries. He is considered to be one of the foremost authorities on success and achievement in the world.

Index